Contemporary Western Design

Contemporary Western Design

HIGH-STYLE FURNITURE & INTERIORS

Thea Marx

Gibbs Smith, Publisher
Salt Lake City

For my daughter, Aspen. May the spiritual journey of creativity bless your life.

First Edition
09 08 07 06 05   5 4 3 2 1

Text © 2005 Thea Marx
Photographs © 2005 as noted on page 160

Published by
Gibbs Smith, Publisher
P.O. Box 667
Layton, Utah 84041

Orders: 1.800.748.5439
www.gibbs-smith.com

Designed by Steve Rachwal
Printed and bound in Hong Kong

Library of Congress Cataloging-in-Publication Data

Marx, Thea.
  Contemporary western design : high-style furniture and interiors / Thea
Marx.—1st ed.
      p. cm.
  Includes bibliographical references.
  ISBN 1-58685-434-8
  1. Interior decoration—West (U.S.) 2. Decoration and ornament,
Rustic—West (U.S.) I. Title.
NK2008.M37 2005
747'.0978—dc22
                                    2005011254

contents

western style redefined

Historically, the West has been known for its rugged landscape, incredible vistas, and natural elements. The architecture, interiors, and furnishings have typically followed suit. Elements found west of the Mississippi have dominated the materials used in the creation of the spaces, usually with the ruggedness with which they were found; that is, they have up until the last decade.

LEFT: *A home is furnished almost completely with the work of artisans from Cody, Wyoming. Chandelier by Peter Fillerup; club chairs and ottoman by Triangle Z Ranch Furniture; dining room table, chairs, barstool, and buffet by Mike Hemry; kitchen barstools by Lester Santos; and hall-way table by John Mortensen.*

Deeply Rooted Console Table *by Santos Furniture.*

The stained-glass portion of the table symbolizes the leaves and berries of the hackberry tree while the lower wood part depicts the trunk and branches. Combining wood, stained glass, and hammered copper for the top, the table is an exemplary display of creativity at its pinnacle. Winner of the Switchback Ranch Purchase Award, the piece is now part of the Buffalo Bill Historical Center's permanent collection.

Western design has evolved from a look easily recognized as rough-hewn lodgepole-pine furnishings, brightly colored leather, and Chimayo weavings to stately pieces that are graceful, elegant, and highly polished, covered in subtle downy soft suede and ornamented with semiprecious stones. The new era of artists and crafts-

Mountain Majesty Chandelier *by Bill and Joyce Feeley.*

The colors of the rising sun reflect on the many elevations of piece of art made from cut steel, stained glass, naturally shed elk antler, rawhide, and mica.

people are designing with a sophisticated flair, unabashedly mixing unusual materials, recycled components, and luxurious fabrics with the beautiful woods that grace the West. The West has always inspired a pioneer spirit and so it goes with those creating pieces that are and will be significant to the daily lives of homeowners in the West or those who choose to live with the West in their hearts.

A globe reminiscent of a Japanese lantern amongst cherry blossoms is created with semiprecious stones and steel, burled wood is set gracefully into the legs of a simple yet sophisticated *Queen Anne Goes*

West Desk, and a contemporary rendition of a horse is formed of molten steel and set quietly on top of an uncomplicated hallway table. A feeling of freedom has motivated the creators of fine western decorative art. Cut steel, Molesworth reproductions, and antler chandeliers are still very much alive and a part of the design realm, but they have a new refined character.

Sun Globe *by Carl Dern Studio with Karen Brown.*

Reminiscent of a Japanese lantern glowing amongst the spring cherry blossoms, this piece is made of citrine, carnelian, peridot, freshwater pearls, and steel.

Wild West Sink and Vanity *by Reflections of Joi.*

Brilliantly disguised as weathered wood, scattered with postcards from Buffalo Bill's Wild West Show, traditional fire clay is the foundation of this charming vanity. The basin is even hand painted to resemble an old metal washbasin.

With meticulous craftsmanship, the western furnishings of today are brilliantly thought out, ablaze with fresh perspective and, at times, delightful humor. Techniques that were previously only applied to furniture pieces have graduated to rudimental components of the home. Built-in dining room cupboards are wrapped in leather, tooled, and adorned with copper earrings; bathroom sinks made of fine china are painted with brands and western panoramas; refrigerators and dishwashers, no longer mundane appliances, are covered in a beautiful cherry burl adorned with elk-horn pulls.

OPPOSITE: *Home theater by DeCunzo Design Associates.*

A full 5.1 surround-sound environment was incorporated into a small home theater without heavy wall treatments. The cabinet is made of hand-carved mahogany and cherry. The ceiling dome is handmade mahogany and black walnut. The piece consists of sixteen individual hand-curved panels and sixteen solid ribs for support. The stain is painted in a delicate scroll pattern near the top to accentuate the antique brass chandelier, recovered from a defunct hotel in Seattle. The different woods vary in density and texture, providing a balanced acoustic signature.

Warmed by hundreds of days of sunshine a year, nothing could be more important to the West than light. From skillful placement of windows to dynamic interpretations of lighting fixtures, the transformation of basic lamps and chandeliers is astounding. Stained glass and parfleche have found their way onto the same grand chandelier, creating a brilliant display of color, light, and mood that angles gently off steel shadows of Rocky Mountain wildlife surrounding the source of illumination. Somewhat resembling the delicate structure of wasp nests, with layer upon layer of tiny glass strips woven with leather bands, these captivating sconces shed soft light onto a silken-finished buffet and matching dining room table done in a "western meets Arts and Crafts" style.

Basket Sconce *by Peter Fillerup of Wild West Designs, and buffet table and chairs by Mike Hemry.*

This sconce hangs perfectly over an Arts and Crafts buffet anchored by Frank Lloyd Wright-esque wall plaques. Made of woven cream glass and leather, this piece has an amazing texture, like a glorious reed basket. Stately and elegant, it throws gentle light over its subjects.

Fancy Dancers *by Cloudbird of Dancing Light Lamps.*

Hand-painted cranes on a rawhide shade inspired the name of this lamp. The piece has a graceful hand-forged steel base as well as Cloudbird's hand-beaded and laced signature work that finishes it eloquently.

Great room design by Barb Cooke of Velvet Leaf Design. Painting above fireplace by Jim Nelson.

Inspired by respect and enthusiasm for the American Indian culture, the owners wanted to create a home that did not portray hunting or fishing. The great room Barb fashioned is elegant and comfortable. The scale of the fireplace, which spans two levels, makes the room feel grand and spacious.

The utensils of daily living found in great rooms, offices, and bedrooms have gathered notoriety not only for their functionality but also for their comfort and beauty. A juniper settee captures the Oscar with its buttery soft leather painted with ledger drawings, while fringe from a hand-carved and beautifully upholstered chaise lounge tickles a hide hand painted with Native American legends. A routine lounge chair sports a personality with spotted cowhide and smooth, supple leather gently but persuasively edged in traditional tacks. A poised, graceful bench, whose seat is appliquéd with pinecones, finds itself at home underneath a Picasso. A sleigh bed made of gentle arches and the rolling curves of colorful juniper fills a bedroom with reassurance of a restful night's sleep. Throwing shadows of western heroes, a fire screen captures the sparks of a dancing fire, which warms the room and glows delicately around the edges with a sense of peacefulness untamed.

ABOVE: *Interior of Copper Camper. The camper brings haute western design onto a new plane. The walls are "papered" with buckskin by Thomas & Son and all metal objects are, of course, copper.*

LEFT: Copper Camper *designed by Hilary Heminway.*

OPPOSITE: *Even the banquette is made of shimmering metal. As usual, Hilary has thought of every detail and each is done to perfection.*

Home by Jerry Capron, with doors by Sun Mountain and sconces by Art, Sand and Steel.

Looking west as the sun sets over the Rockies, a set of double doors opens gracefully into a Wyoming home. The home captures the ruggedness of the local terrain but is softened by the light of glowing copper sconces with wild horses running across hammered surfaces.

Outside, the architecture has gone beyond log and stone to deeply patinated steels, glowing copper, recycled wood aged to perfection, and textured concrete. Welcoming entries are complete with leaded glass. Dramatic doors and warm woods are lighted with copper sconces found first in Africa and then rethought for the West. Antler chandeliers and antique lanterns complete the room.

Contemporary furniture companies have recently discovered great value in the West. In an effort to capture the restfulness of the western state of mind, some North American furniture companies have begun to create western lines, interpreting the style of western craftspeople and artists into consumer lines that allow everyone the chance to enjoy the spirit of the West.

This book is dedicated to the brilliance of the craftspeople, men and women who share their souls with us each time they create a work of art. A piece of western design is never measured in the hours that it took to create, but rather in the number of heartbeats, sunrises, and sunsets from conception to the final moments of repose before life.

Sunset Cocktail Table from the Sun Valley Collection by Century Furniture.

When American settlers moved west, they used the plentiful woods available in the West to create barns and homes. The curved trusses they often used for roof support were based on European forms. This cocktail table is inspired by those trusses and the craftspeople who created decorative inlay surfaces.

Chimayo chest from the Sun Valley Collection by Century Furniture.

Inspired by ancient Native American weavings and rugs, this chest can be a centerpiece in any room. The convex and concave moldings symbolize Chimayo tribal themes.

Lodge Bed *from the At Home in the High Country Collection by Drexel Heritage Furniture.*

Evoking the grandeur of the Rockies, the Lodge Bed is eloquently detailed without being overdone and powerful without losing its integrity. It perfectly matches the wildness and simplicity of the high country.

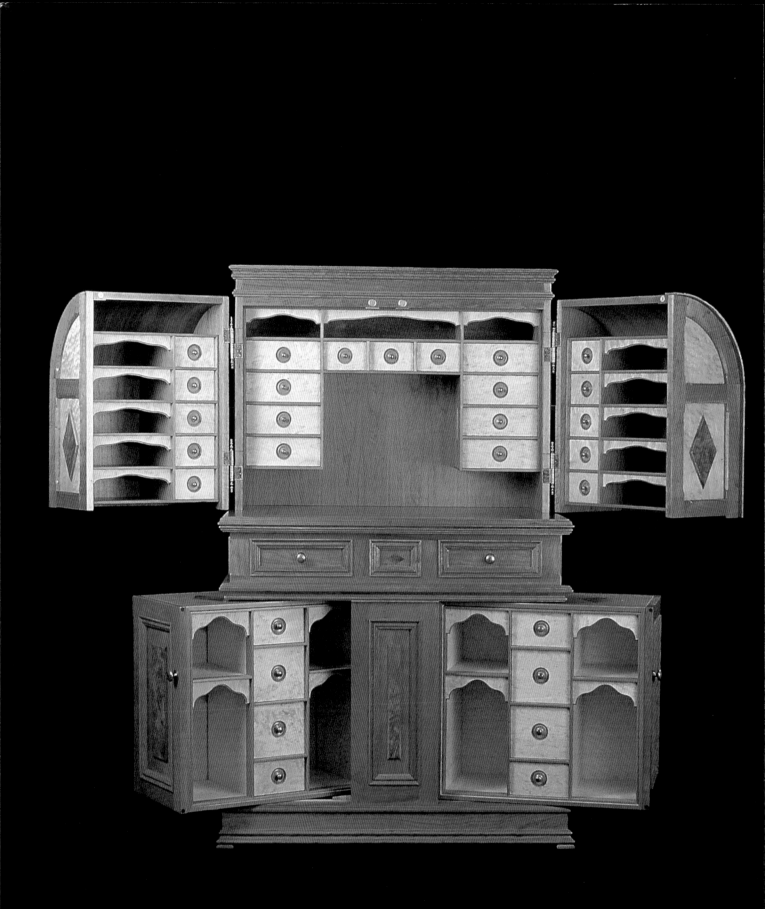

noteworthy pieces

Western craft has evolved into a genre singularly recognizable by its lines
and the materials used in its construction. It has attracted an attentive audience who anticipates, with
bated breath, the next piece, next design, and next brilliant combination of landscape and structure.
Exceptionally talented western craftspeople are driving this evolution.

Rotary Writing Cabinet *by Don Rawlings.*

*A person with gnarled hands and endless arthritic pain is not who you envision when you first see Don
Rawling's signature. It is a flowing, eloquent, and elaborate handwritten script. Nevertheless, his work is
as mesmerizing as his signature.*

*The Rotary Writing Cabinet was inspired by furniture styles circa the 1870s—more specifically the
famous Wooton Cabinet Secretary of 1874. The Wooton was known as the king of desks and was
owned by many prominent nineteenth-century personages—bankers, lawyers, physicians, and railroad
promoters, including John D. Rockefeller, Ulysses S. Grant, Joseph Pulitzer, and Queen Victoria.*

*The Rotary Writing Cabinet is primarily constructed of black cherry, with white birch and oak used as
secondary woods. The nineteen raised panels and twenty-nine inlay motifs are of Carpathian elm burl
polished to a high sheen. The drawer fronts and valances are of splendid bird's-eye maple. The Rotary
Writing Cabinet, once made for the upper crust of society, has been reborn and adapted for technology
and for a new generation of aristocracy with help from the brilliant hands of a master.*

*The base of the cabinet opens by rotary pivot, giving access to the entire interior, which contains shelves
and cubbies for file storage and drawers for CDs and miscellaneous items. The upper radius doors open
to give wide and full access to the twenty-one drawers and fifteen shelves. Separating the base from the
upper section are two deep, fully extending desk drawers with four trays. Inlay dots and points in the top
and swing-outs are mother-of-pearl. Somewhere there is a secret door, which opens with a magnet, that
only the owner knows how to access.*

Leatherwork detail on Carla's Hutch.

Carla's Hutch *by Chapman Design, cabinetry by Grand Woodworks, and interior design by Marianne Bortz Interior Design, Inc.*

Created as a centerpiece for a Colorado home, Carla's Hutch *was a "beautiful collaboration between the owner, cabinetmaker, and myself," said Chris Chapman, who took the owner's sketches, her thoughts and dreams, and created a piece whose visual rhythm set the tone for its mesmerizing existence. The substantial hutch is eighteen feet long and over nine feet high. It grounds the kitchen with a melding of old Eastern European roots and Chris's signature leather-wrapped design. A virtuoso with beaming talent, Chris has never been afraid of crossing into uncharted territory, creating high-relief carvings that leap to life off the panels in a technique similar to creating metal repoussé.* Carla's Hutch *is an articulate demonstration of Chris's talent with its exquisite panels and drawers, high-relief carvings, and nouveau family crest.*

Carla's Hutch *was built to be passed down through the generations, becoming historically significant to heirs and holding priceless sentimental value. It will evoke memories of holidays spent in a special home created for family time.*

Festive Lady *by Amber Jean.*

Many times pieces are created because of a craftsperson's spiritual experience that has awakened the senses and sent electrical responses flying through the creative nerves.

Amber's immense talent, steeped in training and education in classical fine arts, has been incorporated into furniture. Amber melded the flowing manes and tails of the expertly carved mares and foals into the gentle motion set forth by the waves of juniper rolling across the head and footboards. Festive Lady is anchored by juniper posts that weathered time long enough to have grown stout in the prevailing winds. The posts hold the lifelike carvings that beg to be touched, explored, and appreciated for their brilliant texture and infinitesimal detail.

For a decade, Amber has been unafraid to reach beyond her wildest dreams of creation. Nothing can deter this Montana sculptor from pushing forward, setting standards, and breaking them—all in one swift motion of creativity and luminous gesture of love toward nature and humankind.

Wild and Wooly *chair and ottoman by Anne Beard.*

Wild and Wooly is a signature piece that now sits in the Buffalo Bill Historical Center, the ultimate home, as the Switchback Purchase Award winner. The piece is Anne's "someday piece"—that piece that an artist dreams of creating if only time will allow. The piece has every single thing Anne's creative mind could possibly think of and apply. "I wanted to cover every surface. I wanted this piece to be a homage to the bucking horse," said Anne. "When the chair wasn't enough, I created a horseshoe ottoman. When one horseshoe ottoman wasn't enough, I created two, and then I put them together to nest."

Anne wanted to create a piece as original as the green colt that throws every rider. She succeeded, and magnificently so! She redefined the traditional ottoman, using the arc of the horseshoe for the shape and applying tedious details, including the rope-embossed, leather-covered legs hidden beneath the fringe with edges laced together in perfection. This deep roasted-pepper red confection was created from the heart of a cowgirl to embrace the symbol of the West in a glorious flourish of color, cherished detail, and zenith of creativity.

High Plains Lounger *by Eric Shell of Spear S. Woodworks with Rhonda Pollat. Switchback Ranch Purchase Award winner at the Western Design Conference.*

Eric Shell created the High Plains Lounger for the toughest exhibition of western design craft in the world, the Western Design Conference. He was a rookie, with a brilliant concept and a feel for the wood he worked with his hands. Low profile and gentle on the eyes, the High Plains Lounger is a simple but defining cross between traditional and contemporary western. Constructed of juniper and cherry and dye stained to a deep wine tone, the lounger's black leather cushions are boot stitched in true western fashion. The knotted and twisted juniper gives way to its heritage of survival on windblown mountainsides. The cherry is sleek, glamorous, and silky to the touch.

Eric's incarnation of creative thought resides as an ode to youthful courage and intrepid spirit in the Buffalo Bill Historical Center as a part of its permanent collection.

Queen Anne Goes West *by Ron and Jean Shanor of Wildewood Furniture.*

The West used to be primarily dominated by masculine nuances. No longer is this the case. Ron and Jean have created a desk so graceful and ladylike that it is truly fit for a queen. Along with its elegantly appointed chair with pearlized-bronze upholstery and lambskin so soft its occupant melts into the seat, the Queen Anne Goes West *desk is a stunning piece of craftsmanship. It has glorious poetic lines, graceful burl inlays, and long, lovely legs, with natural cabriolets, curved gently by nature herself. This authoritative piece needs no further accessorizing to make a finely dressed lady royalty.*

Close to nature and always appreciative of the bounty that she gives, Ron and Jean have long been the ultimate creators of furniture that incorporates burls found in the lodgepole forests around Cody, Wyoming, where they reside. The two artisans skillfully create pieces from nature's burls, which are formed by a symbiotic relationship between the pine borer beetle's larvae and the lodgepole pine. The Shanors' art furniture is both dynamic and skillfully crafted. Their pieces are absolute masterpieces from the heart of nature's bounty.

Night Fishing *by Carl Dern Studio with Karen Brown.*

Fluid. Enchanting. Daring. Minimalist in its structure and magnificent in the intrigue that it evokes, Night Fishing *is a personal expression of Carl Dern's memories of Cottonwood Creek near Salt Lake City, Utah, where he swam, rafted, and fished as a twelve-year-old boy.*

The collaboration between Carl and Karen to create this striking piece is an obvious testament to a good mix. The energy of the creek's cascading water is symbolized in the twisted copper rod, and the idea of fishing at night on the stream is expressed in the bare bulbs of the piece. The white jasper stones suspended beneath the surface by tiny wires evoke the image of fish roe in clear water.

Moose Country Chandelier *by Bill Feeley.*

Moose Country *is made of cut steel, traditional forged steel, and mica.*

Bill's extraordinary experiences from years in the wilderness and his intimate love of wildlife combined with his unbelievable artistic ability give him the edge. His realistic representations of North American big game are unmatched, and his ability to transfer his experiences to steel is evident in his masterful creations.

Rogue River Chandelier *by Cloudbird of Dancing Light Lamps.*

Imagine a beautiful chandelier earring dangling, catching the light, intriguing the audience with its simple tiered loveliness. Apply the same principle to the Rogue River Chandelier, a timeless piece that could light a stone-castle foyer or hold its own in a rustic lodge. Built on a canopy body with enclosed center pipe, this jewel's hanging system is a lovely cascade of hand-forged leaves. The canopy is surrounded with cranberry amber handblown glass globes of borasilicate, a glass that holds many natural metals that provide color and clarity. The glass is very strong, lightweight, and heat resistant. The globes rest gently on hand-forged five-leaf fitters from which natural quartz crystals dangle, held in place by leather-wrapped, beaded armatures.

The chandelier is very versatile and can be adapted to fit any room. It can hold six to thirty-six globes and can be hung three to twelve feet from the ceiling. Cloudbird has done a delightful job of integrating materials to create a piece that is as curvaceous as it is statuesque. It is elegant with strength and vulnerability but also smart. It is indeed a gloriously functional piece that fills a room with effusive light.

Interior of Ridge House *bridge.*

Ridge House *at daybreak by Olson Sundberg Kundig Allen Architects.*

Leaving the earth and timber on the undulating hillside untouched, Ridge House *respects the land, gives way to its natural light patterns, and embraces the revered landscape. As Tom Kundig notes, "The critical underlying idea of the project was its intention to lightly float the individual rooms along the natural landscape ridge. The bedrooms are a string of pearls that bridge and lightly touch the land. Our strategy allowed the natural landscape to be left undisturbed and opened the interior spaces to the pine forest with views to a stream valley and horse meadow on either side of the ridge. In essence, we constructed a tree house!"*

The occupants of this house enjoy the wilderness not only from above but also from amongst its undisturbed beauty. The house offers a dreamer the perfect refuge to watch the heavens at night or the forest as it comes to life at daybreak.

Circular Sectional *by Jimmy Covert. Metalwork by John Simmons and upholstery by John Robinson.*

Filling a space immersed in both western and old Hollywood history with an appropriate piece that matches the decor and feel of the room could be intimidating but not for Jimmy Covert. Jimmy is a quiet master of the gallant furnishings of the West. With an impeccable sense of style and innate ability, Jimmy creates pieces that make a room feel good.

Taking two years, Jimmy produced the circular sofa for Bill LaWarre's ranch near Fishtail, Montana, which has seen the likes of Clark Gable and other Hollywood A-listers over the past century. Its half-circle design embraces the stone fireplace, consciously circling the warmth and creating an area perfect for long conversations. The arrowhead tables bring their tips into the circle, drawing energy into the center. The steel lamps provide illumination after the sun sets over the Absaroka Range, and the old lodge starts to relive its colorful past.

western whimsy

The West, with its wide-open spaces and natural beauty, is an ideal environment for craftspeople. Communication is still at a premium in some western locales today—sometimes as a result of people's choices and sometimes because of government issues. Along with space and time, the West has granted artisans the freedom to go beyond the norm and work outside the boundaries. The West dares craftspeople to try to interpret Mother Nature's sense of humor.

The West is known for its characters, those who can tell hilarious stories. Their antics are so outlandish and bizarre that you shake your head, wondering if such feats are even possible. Their legends are so extravagant that your sense of awe is inspired.

Western artists have a knack for capturing the sense of these characters in grandiose pieces created with humor beyond your wildest imagination. They also craft modest pieces that feature subtle details that bring to life the struggles of life in the West—struggles that can be met only with humor, as any other response would be inappropriate.

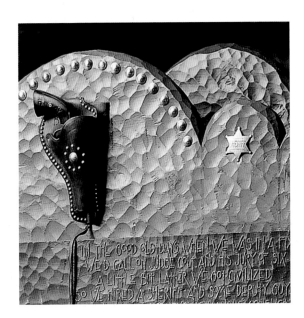

Judge Colt Trastero *by L. D. Burke.*

L. D. is one of the West's most brilliant whimsical artists. Without fail, his pieces make you giggle, inhale sharply, or stop and stare as their impact settles into your bones. Using found objects, a rainbow of color, lively texture, and shapes, his work, recognizable even from afar, is oh-so-welcome in our serious world.

Alamo Gun Cabinet *by Jerry van Vleet of Legendary Heirloom.*

Jerry's small custom-built armory cabinet is a sportsman's dream. Able to hold fourteen rifles, five fly rods, and twelve pistols, all items are locked securely and ready for use on demand. Not only is the gun cabinet hefty in size but also in material; it is made of black walnut and stucco with patinated, galvanized steel from an old barn. This creative, functional, and formidable piece also has real cactus accents.

Cameo Horses *by Anne Beard.*

In this piece, Anne has captured a true sense of a cowgirl's love of her horse. Anne's one-of-a-kind footstools and chairs reflect this talented tailor's sense of style, dazzling use of fine fabric, and artistic interpretation of a cowgirl's West. Anne's sense of color, attention to minute detail, and loving consideration of each stitch makes her pieces simply divine and loved by the cowgirl in all of us.

Pat's Pull Toy, *a functional cocktail table, by Pat Olson Sculpture & Furniture Art.*

Pat can always delight an audience with his creations of metal, glass, and stone. In this piece, Pat incorporated cut steel into layers, creating a horse whose varying elevations give depth, texture, novelty, and uniqueness while it glides along to its chosen location on hand-cut gold wheels.

Chestnut Horse Stool *by R. C. Hink.*

Hand-carved and hand-painted, the Horse Stool is one of R. C.'s humorous pieces. R. C. has the unique ability to make whatever he carves so lifelike that a double take is in order just to make sure it's wood and not a slicker draped over a chair or a saddle on its stand.

OPPOSITE: Art Nouveau Meets the West *by Hone's Design Studio.*

Long, arduous drives across the deserts and prairies of the West fostered many a western tale and brought many new faces to an unexplored land. The longhorn steer in this piece peers through the scrub brush and cactus as though guarding his shady spot for just a few more moments before the cowboy pushes him on toward his destination. Ornately carved, this cabinet's whimsy captures the spirit of the West's romance and struggle.

Outlaw Cabinet *by Greenwood Designs.*

A stunning dry-bar cabinet by Brad Greenwood houses a state-of-the-art diorama, which is brought to life by the drop of a quarter. Look closely at this three-dimensional scene and notice the saddle, snake, tarantula, and cigar, along with other details. The cowboy is a moving, talking robot sitting in front of a saloon filled with silhouetted dancers. The show is lively with sound, lights, and moving characters. Brad engineered and wired the robotics, lights, and electrical components, and his wife, Lorraine, programmed the sound and animatronics.

The details don't stop with the diorama but continue throughout the cabinet itself. Handmade miniature wooden wagon wheels and metal horseshoes adorn the crown molding, while hand-textured edges grace the doors, viewing area, and pull-out serving board. A shelf for glasses with a tiny barbwire fence and a leather coin pouch to catch the quarters is in the lower cabinet.

OPPOSITE: Cowgirl Entertainment Center *by Ranch Willow Furniture.*

Creative and resourceful beyond belief, Lynn Sedar Arambel has created a dynamite entertainment center using a 1949 Willeys Jeep door, the window rolled down to reveal the television behind. When rolled up, the painted window by Nancy Witzeling shows off a cowgirl as she drives to town in her vintage mode of transport. When opened, the door reveals historic brands carved into leather by the world-famous King's Saddlery on its interior and cubbyholes galore. The center is creative and fun while also functional. The top portion can be removed from the bank of drawers and set on antique claw feet, or it can be used as a bar while the drawers function as a bureau.

kitchens

Fresh ideas, like fresh ingredients, are dominating the kitchens of the West.
Once a very sterile room used only for food preparation, design wasn't imperative. In contrast, today's kitchens are being paid homage for playing an important role, beyond simple subsistence, in our everyday lives. Kitchen walls are decorated with beautiful art. Labor-intensive cabinetry, adorned in exemplary fashion, serves as a purposeful and substantial kitchen furnishing. Sinks of copper, hand pounded in delightful patterns and rich textures, complement faucets so striking they could be called jewelry. Appliances that were once humdrum are now covered in gorgeous woods, leather, and metal. Where standard handles once reigned supreme, antler, porcelain, and hand-forged pulls, as well as crystal handles now take their place. Today, kitchen floors are made of distressed historical woods recovered from aging buildings, handmade tiles, slate, and dyed concrete.

In a dynamic splash of color, this kitchen in Montana is suited for hard work and good conversation. Western sunrises often wear red halos in a dramatic opening curtain to the day. This kitchen's repertoire is nothing short of dramatic. With rouge and bleu outre-mer mamboing on the backsplash tile and red-as-red-can-be resin barstools striking poses amongst mosaics of trees, sky, and black granite, this kitchen is not for the fainthearted. It is lively, fun, and oh so va-va-va-voom western.

Lichen hanging from a tree is where this eccentric, yet blissful, room began. "This color is what the kitchen cabinets should be," the owner proclaimed, showing the moss to Chris Neill of North Country Woodworks. Chris went to work creating a stain to match the kitchen to the lichen. The counter is poured concrete, the blue-green color of the North Sea with an exposed polished aggregate surface.

Panels in the cabinet doors are made from local slate. On the bar face, colorful rocks, fossils, and semiprecious stones are embedded in the mosaic of the aspens that look over the mesmerizing terrain.

The tile work in the kitchen was created by Sarah Anderson of Thirsty Lake Tileworks. Sarah was inspired by the freedom with which she was allowed to create and by the owner's boundless energy. Rocks, shells, coral, and found treasures collected from travels afar are strewn across the countertop and embedded into the concrete. "Every time I eat, I relive my life and the places in the world my wife and I have traversed," explained the owner. "Freedom equals beauty."

The kitchen has become the gathering place and, as such, is worthy of decoration. Many times a party graduates without apology to the kitchen to visit, to watch the cook work, and to soak in the delightful aromas and action that come with the ritual of preparing food. There is color, texture, and variety everywhere in modern kitchens.

Dining rooms were once separate from the kitchen area, situated in a place that was elegant and full of repose, far from the clinking and clanking of pots and pans. Today, however, dining rooms are very much a part of the whole food experience, integrated into the same space as the kitchen, perhaps separated only by a bar or a change in flooring. Dining rooms can be open, inviting, casual, elegant, rustic, or chic. All in all, they are meant to be used every day and enjoyed.

Western dining rooms are not reserved for holidays or special occasions. They are hardworking rooms that are used every day. The dining experience in the West is always a festive gathering of families reconnecting and relaxing after separate morning departures. Rarely, however, are western meals reserved for just family. I remember when I was growing up that anyone within two miles of the house when a meal was served was invited. There was always enough to eat, and if you happened to show up at mealtime, you got fed. My mom was an incredible cook and her feelings were hurt if you were there but didn't

join in. The same carries over into my house today: food is celebration and always an open invitation for conversation and good company.

Cabinet by Santos Furniture.

The strokes from the paddles hardly disturb the water in the painting that is the focal point of this juniper and cherry cabinet. Stunning in its quiet brilliance, the cabinet, with its cupboards and drawers, is the epitome of "beauty meets functionality."

Dining room table by John Gallis of Norseman Designs West with chairs by Marc Taggart & Company.

Made of Douglas fir, this Molesworth-style round dining table, with two twenty-four-inch leaves, can expand to feed a whole crew of hungry travelers. The elegant table is flanked by armchairs made of red antiqued ox hide with gold leather fringe and piping. There are eight layers of material in the seats for ultimate comfort. The arrows and whirling log symbols are gold to match the fringe.

Rustic Kitchen *by Bill Coffey and Russ Gleaves.*

Adirondack design inspired Bill and Russ as they embarked on the task of creating a defining kitchen in a Wisconsin home. The shapely custom cabinetry made from fourteen kinds of wood and beautifully trimmed in twig work exemplifies the use of natural forms with fine curves and gentle slopes. Burls, usually found on the legs of furniture pieces, are balancing points for the curves. The handblown leaded-glass doors reveal the cabinets' contents. Looking out onto snow-covered terrain, the room's windows are rimmed in delicate valances of birch bark with scenes of fall painted in their centers. The kitchen is warm, inviting, and unafraid of the rigors of creating artful meals.

Dining room by Harker Design.

Providing an array of different ambiances for a room whose popularity cannot be mistaken, elaborate ironwork frames the inset lighting overhead in this exquisite dining room. With the warmth of a fire, comfortable furnishings, and the spirit of beautiful craft, this room welcomes its guests with Rocky Mountain splendor.

Medicine Wheel Dining Room Table *and built-in cupboards by Chapman Design.*

This leather-wrapped table stands before built-in cupboards that are tooled, adorned with copper earrings, and also wrapped in leather. The granite counter anchors the stunning piece for optimum functionality in a Wyoming home.

Detail of Medicine Wheel Dining Room Table.

Uncle Billy's Iron Mine *dining set by Quandary Design, Inc.*

The glass-topped table has tooled and distressed saddle-leather panels, an antiqued steel base, and a patinated copper apron. The chairs are made with an antiqued steel frame, saddle leather, copper aprons, and a steel accent strip.

Dining room designed by Gunnar Burkland of G2. Fire screen by Gilmore Metalsmithing. Home built by George Schaeffer.

The fireplace is indeed the focal point of this dining room. The custom fire screen, with stylized grape-leaf overlay, is a beautiful complement to this well-designed home.

Kitchen by Copper Creek Canyon.

Copper, the metallic element that brought electricity and communication capabilities to the western frontier, adds warmth and brilliant depth to a kitchen created by Copper Creek Canyon of Indianapolis. The kitchen, with its earthy textures and abundant colors, embraces the distressed, dramatic black cabinetry of the bar set amongst copper elements whose pristine surfaces were fired by Twisted Steel to get a delightful brindled patina. Bordeaux granite countertops, hand-forged corbels, and halogen lighting complement the custom cabinets made of wormy maple finished with hand-rubbed oil and black glaze by Zinn Kitchens, the hand-pounded copper farmer's sink, and the diverse yet dynamically matched barstools by Old Hickory Tannery. A tile backsplash hangs behind the stove, while a slate backsplash with bronze inclusions encircles the rest of the working area. Functional, beautiful, and artfully bound by color, texture, and purpose, this is a kitchen enjoyed by both the cook and the guests.

great rooms

How can you be so sure that a great room is western? Just take a look around and feel yourself immersed in the spiritual awakenings of craftspeople who pour their hearts and souls into the pieces that their hands touch for endless hours. Feel the sadness they experience when a piece leaves their shop to be placed in a home. Feel their unspoken sense of giving a part of themselves away. Will the piece have a good home? Will the owners caress the edges and polish the handles of the work of art? Will they appreciate the tears that were shed and the frustration of creative blocks? Feel the relief artisans experience when they know the owner is the right person for a piece.

The options are broad when it comes to defining a great room as western. But we do know a few things. Great rooms in particular are capable of holding many pieces created by individual hearts and souls, bringing nature (however defined) inside, and celebrating the freedom of individuality that we all cherish. Great rooms are just that: great in surface and space and great for conversation, laughter, and fun. These rooms are for serious meetings of the minds and for leisurely gatherings filled with love and family. Western great rooms can be chic, refined, brash, or overstated. There are no limits.

Great room with fire screen doors by Glenn Gilmore.

The large set of doors uses pinecones, branches, and needles for design themes. The frame is of textured bark and the latches are created to resemble branches. Each pinecone consists of approximately forty separate scales forged from three different sizes of round steel. The fire screen doors are scribed to fit the stonework.

Juniper and cherry rocker with quilted leather cushion by Spear S. Woodworks.

Chairs, table, and magazine rack by Marc Taggart & Company. Fire screen by Archive Designs.

In a home in the Pacific Northwest, two matching Molesworth-style burl club chairs and ottomans are delightfully comfortable with reversible ultra-down cushions done in antiqued red ox hide with contrasting gold ox-hide fringe and piping. The arrow fire screen is made of forged steel, with a steel-mesh screen, hammered-copper panels, and copper rivets.

Saddle Chair *and* Wild Pole Lamp *by New West.*

The chair is covered in contrasting leather, with leather-whipped, stitched edges and conchos with leather tassels tied with bleed knots. The lamp has a cut-steel shade lined with rawhide. An applied pole base features a carved western scene.

Simple Chair *by Mark Koons.*

Chosen to represent the Furniture Society in the traveling exhibition, which illustrates curved contemporary studio furniture, this piece is highly unique. Mark's initial inspiration came from an administrator's chair constructed by Josef Hoffmann over a century ago. Mark reinterpreted the original design, which was meant to be a manifestation of authority, making his version more relaxed and comfortable.

Built-in bar with copper sink by Mike Elliott of Western Designs.

Mike remodeled this alcove, once a dressing room in a ski home, into a wet bar. He completed the project by paneling the walls with cedar barn wood, a wineglass rack, and corner shelves. The temperature-controlled wine cellar slides into a barn-wood- and walnut-trimmed shell. A copper faucet and sink sit in a two-inch-thick black-walnut top. The door fronts and drawers are decorated with teak borders, hand-hammered copper corners, and inlays cut from one-fourth-inch stock woods—purple heart, quartersawn oak, maple, walnut, wenge, ebony, red mahogany, Pao Ferro, red oak, and cedar. The handles and drawer pulls are hand carved from piñon pine.

Low-Back Moose Chair *by MacPhail Studios.*

The winner of the Best of Show award at the Western Design Conference, the Low-Back Moose Chair inspires a hunter to head into the wilderness again for another adventure. The chair's frame and arms are made of moose antler, and the body of the chair is covered in elk hide.

Rodeo Daze Chairs, Burl Leg Dry Sink, Indian Paintbrush Magazine Rack, *and* Corner China Cabinet *by New West.*

Made of pine and burl pole, Rodeo Daze Chairs *feature carved and hand-painted rodeo scenes of a calf roper and a pair of team ropers with colorful Chimayo weavings for the seat and back.* Burl Leg Dry Sink *features a copper top, slab front, and antler pulls. The cabinet locks and has an adjustable shelf.* Indian Paintbrush Magazine Rack *shows off Wyoming's state flower in painted carvings and offers plenty of space with three shelves.* Corner China Cabinet, *with birch with wormwood trim, features adjustable glass and wood shelves.*

Bench by Jeffrey Benedetto.

Made from used leather machinery belts, the leather straps used to create this bench have not lost their integrity but have gained character as a result of their color and texture. This dynamic example of craftsmanship and creativity using recycled materials is a tribute to an extraordinary artist.

Sioux Dog by Troy Evans of Block Horse Designs.

This piece is the first in a series of four based on the imagery of Native American pictograph cave drawings. The organic nature of the brown oak embraces the depth of nature's beauty while the lines of the ebonized-mahogany base create continuity between tribal symbolism and contemporary sculpture.

Gunfighter Armoire *and Molesworth-style fringed table by Marc Taggart & Company.*

The gunfighter takes a stance amidst his remuda of horses on an entertainment center. This dynamite and very large piece of furniture has great red-leather detail held in place by hammered nail heads just like Thomas Molesworth used. The drawers and cabinets have large elk-horn burr pulls for easy opening.

Cowgirl Cupboard *by Diane Ross.*

Every busy person needs a beautiful, functional cupboard with splendid texture and rich color. Chip-carved willow designs decorate the alder frame and complement the diamond willow accents of the Cowgirl Cupboard. The cupboard also has a hidden velvet-lined drawer, for those special keepsakes, and a place to hide the key.

Louis in the Forest *by Carl Dern.*

This console table represents how artists and designers of the Louis period of design abstracted the fauna and flora found in nature and brought them into the homes and palaces of kings and queens. Carl used sticks, branches, and twigs to make cast-bronze parts to construct a table in one of the traditional forms of that time. He patinated the surfaces to appear to be aged wood, as if gathered from the forest and assembled on the spot.

Elsie, the Chair *by Tim Groth.*

Aptly named for its gorgeous hair-on upholstery and soft nubuck arms, this is the kind of chair that is comfortable, familiar, and always welcoming. Lodgepole and twisting pine make up the posts and legs while driftwood, cedar, juniper, and twisting pine are used for the applied pole design on the front.

Ranch Settee *by Custom Leather Saddlery.*

A cowboy's delightful interpretation of the classic Victorian settee, this piece is very feminine with its curves yet it has a mighty presence. It is made of hair-on cowhide with a striking yoke, both front and back, and deeply carved leather. Soft, buffed leather covers the arms and sides. The settee is balanced solidly on graceful steer horns. Brass tacks finish the settee, which was the winner of the Best of Show award at the Desert Caballeros Western Museum.

American Black Walnut Cabinet *by SAR Furniture.*

In this unique work of art, hand-carved trees stand out at the corners of the cabinet with leaves and branches growing out and over the crown molding. An eagle with outstretched wings surveys the wilderness landscape below. More than two dozen animals can be found on the cabinet.

Sitting room in a home built by LaChance Builders. Twig work by Diane Ross and totem by Carl Muggli.

In a sitting room off of the children's bedrooms, a warm fire burns, keeping the space warm and comfortable for little feet. The denim chairs are a hardy choice for this room that is often filled with activity. The twig work above and around the fireplace creates an ambiance filled with wonder and an open door for imaginations to run rampant.

Blanket Armoire *by Mike Elliott of Western Designs.*

Mike created an illusion of a colorful Native American blanket on the front of this armoire. There are over 1,475 inlays of nine naturally colored hardwoods that create the design. The wood for this painstakingly constructed piece was collected from an old hay barn and the white-streaked accents are from the old picket fence in front of it.

Diamond Drawer Side Table *by Doug Tedrow of Wood River Rustics.*

Doug never ceases to amaze the eye with his intricate work. In this side table, he balances his reoccurring chip-carved theme to perfection, constructing a piece that is striking and elegant while maintaining its rustic roots.

An "Occasional" Letter Writer's Desk by Big Creek Furniture.

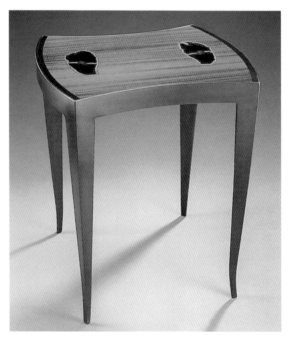

Flared-Arc End Table *by Chajo.*

Great room design by Mary Margaret Interior Design.

You can feel the spirit of the Old West as the chandelier and art meld into a cavalry of bronze. Definitely western, obviously comfortable, and meant to be lived in, this space invites you in, asks you to take your coat off, and motions for you to settle by the fire.

Home built by Preschutti Construction. Home design by Elliott Brainard with interior design by Robin Stater of Sierra Design Studio.

Perched high above the glittering city lights of Mammoth Lakes, California, this grand cabin's great room has several conversation areas. This spot is the perfect place for a family to spend a snowy winter evening enjoying each other's company.

Brindle Mirror *by Stephen Bryer.*

Brindle Mirror *isn't just an accent piece; it is a statement. With brindle hair on hide, the mirror is full of texture. Since it is framed in alder, it is durable yet beautiful. This mirror won Best Artist Accents award at the Western Design Conference.*

Somethin' Fishy *hall table and torchère by Wildewood Furniture.*

The table has naturally bent cabriolet legs, a maple top, birch-bark sides, and a hand-carved fish on the backsplash. The torchère's stem is one piece with a natural burl and rawhide shade.

Bar by Chapman Design.

This bar features a floral Victorian pattern deeply carved into its leather-wrapped front. The kitchen is separated from the great room by this gently curving masterpiece. The goal is for everyone in the house to enjoy meals and delightful conversations either at the bar or seated in a comfortable spot.

bedrooms

Do you hear the creek—jumping, running, frolicking in the night with the
stars twinkling overhead? The stillness beyond is punctuated only by the creatures of the night. The enclave
is a wall tent made of sturdy canvas, its comfort palpable in the vast wilderness. There are no feather beds
to burrow into or lamps to flick on, but rather bedrolls strewn across the meadow floor with flashlights
tucked neatly under pillows. The midnight nature call to the privy is not answered by tired bare feet on
plush carpet, but by bare feet hurriedly stuffed into worn cowboy boots and shuffled across uneven earth.

No matter what comforts we enjoy, there is something primal, comforting, restorative, and reju-
venating about experiencing nature firsthand. It's about the open flames of a fire; a bedroll warming to
your body, chasing away the chill of the mountain air; and the togetherness that is created when all hands
help prepare breakfast over the campfire, do dishes in the creek, and remove the hobbles from the horses.
In a particularly special way, the West has brought out the comfort, relaxation, and centeredness that so
many seek in this world that moves at a record pace.

In the bedrooms of the West, we are infused with nature. We are reminded of the nights we have
spent in the open air, the view of the Milky Way with its untethered stars shooting in all directions. Beds
of rolling burl, oscillating juniper, and sleek aspen proclaim prominence in western bedrooms. Sleek,
hearty, wholesome, and beautiful bedrooms in the West are as unique as they are welcoming.

Rocky Mountain Bed *by Chapman Design.*

In a cross-culture mix of classic European and Spanish territorial design, this bed balances the feminine and
masculine energies of delightful western details. The essence of majestic mountain ranges establish their
presence on the head and footboards while a herd of grazing cow elk watch an approaching bull intently.

Mariposa Bedroom Suite *by How Kola.*

Understated elegance with a touch of Molesworth style and twenty-first-century technology come together in this bedroom set. The king-size bed, made of pine and poplar, has a spoon-gouged head-board that lends glorious texture to the finish. The bed was designed in concert with the owner and features the ranch's brand. It is finished with a leather band and tacks on the headboard and footboard in true Molesworth style. The matching nightstands hold decisively western lamps with Taos shades. The cut-steel bear lamp is by Ken Cooley. The carved credenza at the foot of the bed is a faux dresser that houses a mechanical center section that brings a television up when activated by remote.

Bedroom suite by Peter Fillerup of Wild West Designs.

In this bedroom suite, burls, which are often such a prevalent part of western style, dictate the design. Easily capturing the flow of each piece, Peter has successfully integrated burls into the bed, nightstands, and lamps. The suite is perfectly matched.

Into the Woods *by COCOPA.*

Into the Woods displays much finesse. It was handcrafted of vintage pine with a mother-of-pearl inlay and hand-forged finials. Though the bed is streamlined, none of the important details have been over-looked. COCOPA expertly melds the modern with the traditional in her own unique way.

Chest of drawers by Barney Bellinger of Sampson Bog Studio.

Five-Drawer High Boy Dresser *by Mike Elliott Western Design.*

The dresser measures thirty-four inches wide, fifty-six inches tall, and twenty-four inches deep. The top is two-inch-thick black walnut with a hand-sculpted edge. The barn-wood face frame is from an old milking barn, located about an hour south of Lake Tahoe. The aspen legs are from Mill Canyon in the Carson-Iceberg Wilderness. The border on the drawers is Peruvian walnut, and the outside of the drawers is inlaid with zebrawood, wenge, curly maple, and lacewood. The inside section is inlaid with red gum wood and cedar barn wood. The drawers are constructed with nine-ply Baltic birch. They are spline jointed and capped with Peruvian walnut. The drawer pulls are made of hand-styled piñon pine roots.

Bed by Chapman Design.

Statuesque in its European-inspired splendor and feminine with graceful, elegant lines, this leather-wrapped bed is neatly carved with hand-tooled details and silver conchos. The pinecones atop each post make the piece at home in the West.

Tall Dresser *by Jimmy Howard.*

*No stranger to hard work or hard play, this dresser is meant to be used,
loved, and passed down through generations of outdoor enthusiasts.*

Home by LaChance Builders.

*Who could resist a quiet evening in this elegantly appointed room with rustic and classic touches?
LaChance Builders has once again created a room where the light adds undeniable warmth, the
fireplace gives off ambiance, and the mirror provides intrigue.*

bathrooms

A far cry from the cold streams, washbasins, and privies of a hundred years ago, today's bathrooms are functional, chic, and fun. They are beautiful, full of texture and color, and perhaps the one place in the house where a busy woman can find respite by locking herself in the steamy room for a long lavender-scented bath in a tub surrounded by handmade tiles, a crackling fire, and a bird's-eye view of the moon as it caps the horizon.

Modern bathroom spaces are infused with nature. Glass of all kinds allows light to filtrate a room that was once relegated to the center of the house, where darkness could be penetrated only by the flip of a switch. Arcing windows, charming skylights, hand-wrought sconces with rawhide shades, stained glass, and a well-thought-out lighting plan are now paramount to the experience of what is becoming one of the most important rooms in the house.

In a contemporary log-home bathroom, the vanity chest is by Old Biscayne and hand painted by Paul Gregory of Mary Margaret Interior Design. The leather-finished mirror is by Chapman Design and the light fixtures are by Roc Corbett. The painting is by Suzanne Baker.

Home by LaChance Builders.

Tile and fireplace design by Mary Margaret Interior Design. Light fixture by Roc Corbett. Iron fire screen and curtain rods by the Iron Thistle Forge.

Bathrooms were once sterile. No longer. They are now infiltrated with touchable and textured accoutrements. River rocks and local limestone surround tubs. Hand-painted tiles and shale and granite, deeply grained and supple, line showers while a curtain of fine buffalo leather keeps water from escaping, allowing ablution. Recycled timber makes floors brawny yet understated. Mirrors are captured in leather, steel, warm-hued woods, and rope. Basins are made of hand-painted china.

Home design by Locati Architects.

Bringing beautiful natural materials inside doesn't necessarily mean a space will be rustic as is the case with this beautiful guest bath. Sophisticated design coupled with deeply grained granite, exquisite hardware, and art glass make this bathroom unique.

Home by LaChance Builders.

This tub, surrounded by local river rock and beautifully etched windows, offers you a chance to relax in an environment mirroring nature but with all the amenities of the good life.

Double Trouble *double sink and vanity by R. Dana Merrill.*

Vanities are cut from slabs of thick juniper, their rough, curvaceous edges left untouched. They are covered in cowhide, rimmed with tooled leather, and balanced on steer-horn legs that have been hand forged into stylish, uncomplicated, essential elements. They are created from antique dressing tables—burls curving, bubbling, dancing with life—and reclaimed wood with silken finishes hand rubbed to earthy hues.

Indeed, gentle summer breezes, sunsets, and the pleasant aroma of sage after a spring shower, wafting through the open windows, aren't just for those who take a dip in the creek anymore. Bathrooms in the West are important to the experience of living in the magnificent region. The West's new rooms of rejuvenation encourage playful excursions just like the frontier does. Rather than a dip in the horse tank as the thunderheads roll in on a hot summer day, a new adventure might now mean a dip in a tubful of splendid bubbles—the only annoyance being unruly bubbles lighting on the end of your nose or the far edge of the gleaming porcelain, just begging to be popped with the toes. Steamy mirrors are perfect easels for purple mountains of majesty or a horse of a thousand colors, basking in the meadow beyond the shimmering panes.

Double-sink vanity and mirror by Randy Edgar of Escargot Fine Woodwork.

An elegantly choreographed double-sink vanity and mirror make a beautiful addition to a log-home bathroom. Randy, an avid outdoorsman, appreciates the bountiful gifts of nature, especially the burls he so enjoys working into his creations. His passion for challenges and desire to keep pushing the envelope has led to marvelous demonstrations of his skill.

Dry Sink by Andy Sanchez.

Andy is a master at taking massive slabs of alligator juniper and turning them into pieces that are useful and appealing. In this refined yet rustic vanity, he has kept the integrity of the wood's rough edges and juxtaposed them with a soft, polished top, creating a piece sophisticated enough to carry off the stained-glass inclusions and the shapely hand-carved basin of alabaster.

Skies of Blue *by Peter Fillerup of Wild West Designs.*

Who needs windows? Peter has created a bathroom that is the outdoors. In his mural, swans and lily pads float on the serene pond amidst the lush meadow in the Rockies. A piece of driftwood lies at its edge, giving you the sense of climbing out of a tent in the wilderness to witness nature's glorious vistas at sunrise. The towels are even hung from the bark of a tree next to the water's edge. A vanity made of applied twigs, stained glass, and a luscious azure basin bring you back to civilization.

The owners integrated the landscape into their consciousness by reflecting the outdoors in their bathrooms. Ceramic artist Benedikt Strebel created the Sonoma Blue and Sonoma Green porcelain tiles by hand in collaboration with McIntyre Tile Company. Sonoma Blue finds its home on the ground floor and represents water. Sonoma Green is situated directly above Sonoma Blue and symbolizes the rolling hills surrounding the California home.

Sonoma Blue.

Sonoma Green.

lighting

Warmed by hundreds of days of sunshine each year, nothing is more important to the West than light. Light determines how we view the different elevations of the glorious landscape, depending on the sun's location in the sky, the clearness of the night, or the strength of the storm. Light turns an ordinary drop of water into a crystal prism, casting rainbows of true color into the atmosphere. Western artists have distinguished themselves by utilizing unique materials for elements of illumination and then melding these materials into sources of light that seize the moment.

As long as we have known earth, light has come in a few rudimentary forms: stars, sun, moon, fire, and, in industrialized times, electricity. Ironically, the most soothing and sought-after light still comes from nature no matter how advanced we become. Western artists are predisposed to working with nature since most of them live a life filled with it. They form concepts and create from its bounty. Calling upon their individual talents, these artists create vessels to throw light, containers to capture and reflect it, objects to deflect it into splendid shadows, and pedestals to flaunt it.

Illumination has the ability to set or alter the mood of a room. Artisans who create light fixtures may be saddled with the task of designing for a corner or a small space over a vanity or for a room of grand proportions. Much like sunlight on a western landscape, the brightness, warmth, or muted tones given off by light fixtures create the sense of the day outside or create a gentler, kinder mood inside. The use of light, whether through sources of illumination or placement of windows, is paramount in creating an enjoyable space, even if it's a small cabin buried in the trees miles from civilization.

Trout Season *by Lean-2 Studio.*

Fanciful and practical, this piece won Best of Show at the Western Design Conference. Trout Season *includes four original paintings; bronze pine, leaf, and acorn details; and a river-stone inlay complete with antique fly-fishing gear, including rods and reels that suspend the bark and twig pendants whose interiors—a canoe seat, backs, and peddles—are made of antique copper. This pieces hangs over a table created by Jimmy Covert and chairs by Lester Santos.*

Aspen Beaver Chew Chandelier *by Peter Fillerup of Wild West Designs.*

Peter Fillerup is best known for his creations of illumination: chandeliers challenged with lighting vast rooms while providing eye-catching art for the occupants to admire. His pieces are diverse and always stunning. But before assuming that a forklift is necessary to move all of his pieces, take note that Peter also has an amazing line of small works of light.

Buffalo Chandelier *by Bill Feeley.*

Whimsical. Straightforward. Real. These words just touch on the work of talented master metalsmith Bill Feeley. Bill's shameless work—hand cut from cold, hard steel with a fiery torch—maintains the integrity of dying art. After years in the saddle and on mountain trails, his humorous take on cowboy life infuses his work with a special spirit. His real-life experiences in the wilderness with wild things show in the chandeliers and lamps he creates with such accurate detail.

Bill draws each pattern freehand and then cuts it without the use of new technology. His hand-forged pieces start as glowing hunks of steel in the pit of an old blacksmith forge, inherited from his grandfather, and become soft and pliable from the strokes of a heavy hammer swung by experienced hands.

Cobweb *by Carl Dern Studio with Karen Brown.*

Artist and sculptor Carl Dern has created one of the era's most charming lighting pieces: a chandelier with three delicate branches cast in bronze and tied with rope as though they were just found adrift in a bubbling brook and then gathered to create this magnificent piece. Strewn about the fragile branches is a web of semiprecious stones: serpentine rock crystal, citrine, peridot, carnelian, calcite, and jasper, all reflecting the wavering light of the real candles with pristine brilliance and giving the appearance of a little girl dancing in the sunshine after finding her way into her mother's jewelry box.

Children's room lighting by DeCunzo Design Associates.

Starlight, star bright . . . Jason DeCunzo created a lighting scheme that dims to starlight over a period of an hour and a half, allowing children time to get ready for bed. The lights automatically dim in the morning as the sun rises. The room is never dark.

In this bedroom built specifically for grandchildren to rest and romp, the owners had DeCunzo's high-tech nightlight system built in so that the children's journey to the potty in the dark of night would not be so daunting. The room itself is a testament to cowboy style. The bunk beds are covered in Indian blankets and curtained in deerskin for a little privacy for those earlier to bed. Hardwood floors with cowhide rugs make upkeep easy, and the steel chandelier complements the bright blue chairs and rugged game table.

Torchère *by Cloudbird of Dancing Light Lamps.*

Cloudbird works diligently to intertwine steel, glass, rawhide, beadwork, and luminosity. Her creations are refined, delicate, and noteworthy. She has taken care to gently combine handblown glass shades, natural crystal, and hand-forged steel. Her hand-beaded accents and wrapped-leather pieces are brilliant and provide warm, beautiful light to a variety of spaces and places.

Cloudbird says, "Light is such an essential element in our lives—it affects the way we feel in our homes; light is so vital to how we live in our spaces, whether it comes through windows or from our lamps. I love to portray light as art—adding ambience and beauty to a room. I love to work with rheostats—placing a dimly lit piece at that place where we sit with our friends for the last part of a lovely evening, or having a special piece on low, sort of a sentinel through the night. My pieces are designed to last lifetimes, to gather appreciation, not be outdated in a decade."

Antler Chandelier, *made of fallow deer antlers, by Doug Nordberg.*

Mission Penrose Chandelier *by Steve Blood of Penrose Company.*

An elegant, unobtrusive piece with Arts and Crafts–style roses, vines, and leaves cut delicately from steel, Mission Penrose Chandelier allows gentle amber light to seep through the cuts and glow from mica while main light is shed through art glass.

Pine Sconce *by Josyln Fine Metalwork.*

Steve Josyln's masterful lighting pieces range from delicate sconces to massive chandeliers. Steve re-creates nature in steel with astonishing detail. A pinecone sconce delivers everything you would wish for without actually accentuating a light with a real pine bough. It seems as though there are a thousand details on one needle.

Pine Tree Sconce *by George Ainslie.*

George's hand forging gives his pieces a life of their own with glorious texture running over their finely cut surfaces. His talent is evident in the Pine Tree Sconce, a simple but stately piece of old-world craftsmanship brought into the twenty-first century.

Archaic Horse *by David LaMure Jr., with handcrafted rawhide shade by Dave Bernstrom.*

Rich in texture and form with subtle details, this beautiful lamp will stop you in your tracks for further inspection.

Three Eagles *by Larry Glaze of Antler Art of the Plains.*

Larry is an environmental artist who uses naturally shed antlers, Osage orange trees, as well as found objects in his work. One of his most sought-after pieces, eagles created from moose antlers with a bronze-patina head and feathers, is in many notable collections, including President George W. Bush's.

The Garden House by Olson Sundberg Kundig Allen Architects. Interior Design by Terry Hunziker.

The house's temple uses light as an instrument of serenity and comfort in a room meant to transport you from the demands of life into a peaceful sanctuary of thought. Subtly reflective wall panels and a curved floating ceiling give the room fluidity to use light to its greatest value. Dominating the temple is a giant steel horse by artist Deborah Butterfield.

Tom Kundig is a master at capturing the warmth and rays of light. He has made a career of creating spaces that have a loving, gentle relationship with the sun and, for that matter, the moon, stars, and great outdoors. His spectacular use of glass creates a sense of being outdoors when you are really protected from the elements. Tom comments, "Light is like the music in a concert hall. It fills and defines the room. It is the reason we experience the room—it's the background and the foreground, the base line and the melody. Of course evening light is equally important. There exists that magic moment when the daylighting from the exterior changes to lighting from the interior, a sort of reverse lantern."

Dahl Sheep Chandelier *by MacPhail Studios.*

Not everything in the West has to be of grand portion to make a statement. Danial MacPhail echoes that sentiment with his low-profile but distinguished Dahl Sheep Chandelier. The four horns are each carved with one of the grand slam's ultimate prizes: the dahl, stone, desert, and bighorn rams.

Express, *made of stained glass and resin, by Kate Tonnessen.*

Vibrant colors wash the sky as the cowboy rides across the prairie. The rider tries to beat the sun's departure from the western sky.

My work should awe," Kate says. "It should cause people's hearts to leap and their breath to quicken. It should elicit the same sensations people would have were they standing in the scene themselves. When this occurs, my art is an understood art."

Window by Stanton Glass.

Appropriately gracing the opening of an arboretum is this window full of gentle motion. Sand-carved leaves drift on a breeze that appears to move across the translucent medium of handblown glass. Bryant and his staff are innovators of light, whether filtered through layers of vibrant stained glass or from exquisite cuts of leaded or bevelled glass void of color but filled with marvelous texture.

Sunroom by Stephen Winer Design.

This whole room of light was built specifically by Stephen Winer to capture the warmth of the sun and hold it gently for its occupants to enjoy. Window seats, rockers, and other comfortable seating make this room inviting. With immaculate details and warmth pervading the room, it's a perfect place to read the morning away, play a competitive game of checkers, or write about the awe-inspiring beauty outside.

libraries and offices

It is said that a house without books is like a room without windows.
Books even in our electronic age are a source of entertainment, learning, and growth. Books are collected, given as gifts, used for work, and cherished as family heirlooms. Libraries offer a personal sanctuary for contemplation and quiet. They are filled with warmth and treasures of past excursions. They are sources for new adventures even if you're traveling will be done in front of the fire, wrapped in a warm soft blanket, with destination details left to the imagination. Furnishings for the library are gentle and conducive to thought. Libraries are quaint and sturdy, rich in texture and detail.

Like libraries, offices are rooms where functionality needs to blend with beauty. Pieces should be touchable, user-friendly, and durable. The space should be bright, pleasant, and conducive to quiet thoughts as well as productive hours.

Some of the West's most talented craftspeople have created the most intimate, charming, humorous pieces for the office. Working from home has become commonplace, with technology allowing you to live and appreciate the West in all its grandeur while furiously chasing stocks around the world. What a wonderful way to live. Offices in western homes are casual, well used, and comfortable. Office space has become a gallery of sorts, featuring beautifully attended-to desks, chairs, and tables made of juniper, alder, maple, and walnut. The desks are finished with lavish details and great flourishes of design: stained glass, intricate carvings, cast-bronze pulls, and surfaces polished to a high sheen and accented with thick leather carved at the edges.

Hallway library by John Gallis. Home designed by Storey Architects and built by Alpine Log Homes, Inc.

There's nothing like a long hallway with walls lined with good books to slow one's pace from frantic to relaxed. The hallway in this home has turned into a virtual library with art, books, and beautiful craftsmanship. John Gallis's bookshelves—made of walnut (with bark still on the edges), spalted maple, and accented with polished antler knobs—adorn the walls and hold treasures literary and found.

Two-Drawer Fly-Fishing Desk *by David Struempler.*

Marquetry is the art of inlaying wood for the purpose of decoration, and no one is better at bringing western life into wood than David Struempler. Using maple polished as smooth as a lake on a calm summer morning, David inlaid the image of a fly fisherman casting into gentle ripples, made ever so realistic by the artful use of the grain. This is a brilliant display of art as furniture.

Chandelier by Antler Art. Design by Mary Margaret Interior Design.

The library in this Arizona home reflects the owner's tastes for fine cigars, classic books, and western art. Earthy, welcoming, and serene, the library is a place for study and deliberation. The fallow deer-antler chandelier is a perfect balancing fixture in the room, shedding light while sparking interest and intrigue in an understated manner.

Executive Decision *by Wildewood Furniture.*

The inspiration behind the Executive Decision *desk was Ron Shanor's desire to create something that a Fortune 500 CEO could sit behind and feel the strength of the position yet experience the calmness and coolness of a peaceful day in the West. The grand desk with a leather inset top with a matching chair claimed Best of Show at the Western Design Conference.*

Spirit Tree Desk *by John Gallis.*

John Gallis has made his name creating desks of magnificent quality and ingenuity. His latest works are starkly contrasted in size but equal in style and craftsmanship. The Spirit Tree Desk is a walnut beauty with juniper trim and is fit for a king or king-size room. Its owner may just imagine he or she is working amongst the trunks, roots, and branches of the forest with all of the twists and turns. Set on a single pedestal, the desk features an oil painting by Guy Rowbury of a starlit night in an Indian village.

Detail of remote-operated compartment inside the Presidential Desk.

Presidential Desk by *Tim McClellan of Western Heritage Furniture.*

Tim McClellan created this desk that is massive in proportions, stately in appearance, and true-grit western design all the way for the Western Design Conference from treasures he collected over twelve years. Salvaged barn wood, a special piece of cherry, wainscoting found in an abandoned miner's cabin, and hand-hammered Indian-head nickels are just a few morsels from his reserve. The desk also has a secret compartment that can surface at the touch of a button to reveal spirits, important papers, or perhaps a forgotten cache.

Calligraphy Desk *by Stephen Winer.*

All details and no fluff, this desk is gorgeous, straightforward, and user-friendly. Made of walnut with purple-heart inlays and accents, which are both raised and flush, this piece makes the flourish of a finely inked pen a joy to behold.

OPPOSITE: Cowboy Chop Suey *by Ed and Diane Grunseth.*

When the West was burgeoning, there was a vast mix of cultures that made the land grow and prosper. Two such cultures were the cowboys and the Chinese who came to this land of new beginnings. Unfortunately, sharing of cultural backgrounds, including art and design, was not allowed or even considered. The fusion took 140 years but this "East meets West" computer desk is one piece in a line of furnishings that have brilliantly integrated the two cultures.

Cowboy Chop Suey is constructed from coffee-stained pine and Douglas fir—both vertical-grain and recycled woods. Inside, there is a writing desk made of Chinese camphor burl wood and a painted scene reminiscent of ancient scrolls. Crossover details complete this fascinating piece: railroad spike locks, drawer pulls and lock plates, a horseshoe sunburst, horseshoe handles, hand-forged metal straps, and studs and nails.

Memories of Grandpa Desk *by Al Hone.*

After gazing at the Memories of Grandpa Desk *for what seems like hours, you will finally believe that you've seen all of the minute and amazing details—that you've touched the fringe on the chaps to see if it moves, or if it's really wood, and that you've found the hidden drawer amongst the pages of one of the books that will carefully hold the round spectacles. Every remarkable detail has been thought of and carved: lantern, pocket watch, quill, and books. The desk is an ode to a lost hero and a tribute to the creativity of Al Hone.*

Lone Bison Desk and Chair *by Brad Greenwood.*

Known for his ability to push the creative limits of his counterparts, Brad created the Lone Bison Desk and Chair *to symbolize the magnificent presence one lone buffalo can have on a person's soul, reminding him or her of the devastation that humankind has wrought out of selfish desire. Built of seven kinds of wood with details of various origins, the oak-sapling round-back supports were bent and pulled taut with rope around large firewood rounds when they were still green. They dried into the perfect shape for the Windsor-style chair.*

details

Without the little things that bring them together, a beautiful home and the
perfect piece of furniture never become part of the greater whole. The little things are details, accoutrements,
accessories, art, and niceties that make an unmistakable difference in how a room feels and looks.

The minutiae may at first seem to play a minor role in the tone of the room visually, but a second
or third encounter will bring them to the forefront of the visual experience. Or, on the flip side, the details
may be so striking that they set the tone immediately. Delightful facets make a room significant in its own
right. Details might include curls, twists, and burls climbing a staircase; a historically correct reproduc-
tion of a Native American dress so vivid with details it awes the beholder; or a hidden bottle of spirits
balanced on steer horns in the most unlikely location.

Western artists are unbelievably creative and resourceful, brilliantly combining textures, colors,
and found objects into pieces that dance with personality and put the sparkle into a room. Door pulls
hand-wrought and elegant, vibrant rugs tufted by hand so that every fiber is perfect, floor cloths painted
with layers of glorious color, doors wrapped in thick leather, mirrors encircled in belt buckles won at
rodeos—these are just a few of the fine and exquisite objects western artists fashion and craft by hand.

I Will Remember You *by Supaya Gray Wolfe of Many Tears.*

*After the death of her friend, Supaya created this beautiful historical reproduc-
tion using a process that Native Americans have employed for centuries. The
dress is made from elk hide. Under the beaded turtle, which stands for long
life, is good medicine, symbols used by Native Americans that they believe
bring good or protection to a person. The turtle is surrounded by the colors of
the four directions. The back of the dress has a turtle shell covered with
rawhide hanging from a beaded strap. A drum and drum beater are included
with this piece. The drum beater is made from an elk bone with a hand-carved
pipestone head for beating the drum. The two hands on the drum represent
the people who touch our hearts during this journey we call life.*

OPPOSITE: Transitional Yei *by Line of the Spirit.*

*Brightening any contemporary western space with vibrant color, this rug is
100-percent handspun, hand-dyed highland sheep wool.*

Running Horses *by MKR Design.*

In this 100 percent wool, hand-tufted rug, MKR has captured the essence of freedom and beauty. Horses—their manes and tails blowing, their heads held high—move gracefully through the desert air.

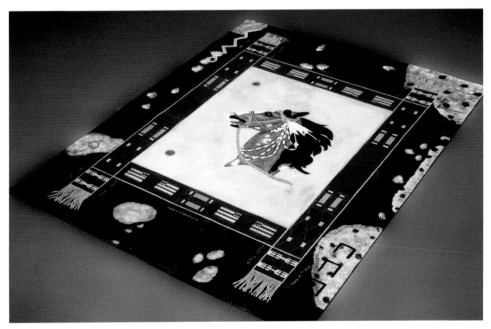

Hand-painted floorcloth by Angie Nelson of Free Rein Studio.

A colorful floorcloth is dedicated to the horses that were so prized by the Plains Indians. "Well respected horses were as well dressed as their riders," explains Angie. A beautiful celebration of color for any floor, the floorcloth is a hand-painted replica of a saddle blanket the Plains Indians used.

Burl Staircase *by Escargot Fine Woodworks.*

The effect of climbing this staircase is charming, something like climbing tower steps in a castle. Even though the staircase isn't curving, its components are alive with burl. Intricate pieces of curvaceous, bubbling wood make up this carefully assembled puzzle.

Doors by Chapman Design. Cabinetry and home by RAM Construction.

Leather-wrapped doors seal a built-in entry closet with stately elegance. The astragal in the middle provides an easy handhold and negates the use of hardware. The doors are fully wrapped with a different tooling and nail pattern inside.

Pillows by Lynda Covert on Tim Groth chairs.

Lynda Covert's pillows are divine. Simply divine. Her pillows are scrumptiously laden with beads in patterns that come to her in the quiet hours of the night as she lies resting, readying herself for another day of careful delegation of color and tiny stitches.

Buckskin curtains with beaded trim by Lynda Covert.

Nothing adds to the warmth of a room like deep chocolate-colored buckskin curtains framed in beadwork. Lynda's meticulous bead-work is just the delicate finish needed in a room full of earthy tones.

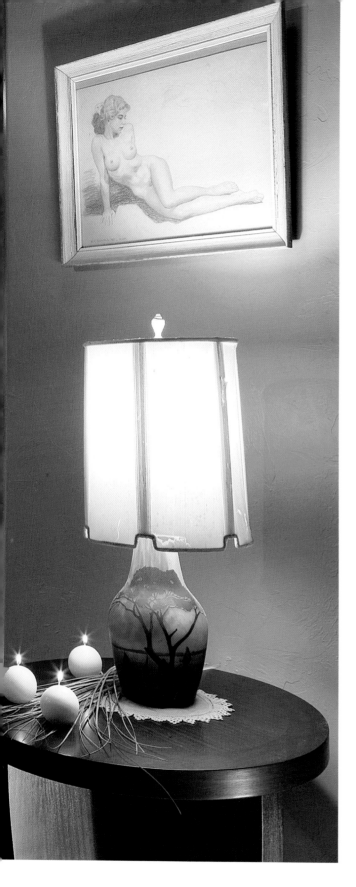

Custom closet by Chris Neill of North Country Woodworks.

Closets are usually created to be used as storage, but are rarely made to be looked at and truly enjoyed. Refined, functional, beautifully lit and accessorized, this closet has his and her sides. Her side allows her to contemplate her reflection in the mirrors inlaid in each of the doors. The bottom third of each cabinet has a different combination of drawers and one big boot drawer. His side has a drawer and a boot drawer under each cabinet. Crafted from walnut, wormy maple, and stainless steel, this closet is delightful inside and out.

Palomino *on gliders by Alan Carr.*

Fit to entertain a child for hours—dancing, prancing, creating wonderment and joy—a child will hold on tight to this pony with her little fingers as her dreams come true. With impeccable craftsmanship; a beautiful finish; and vivid details, including a real mane and tail, tooled saddle, and bridle, the gliding horse is a striking feature in a child's room.

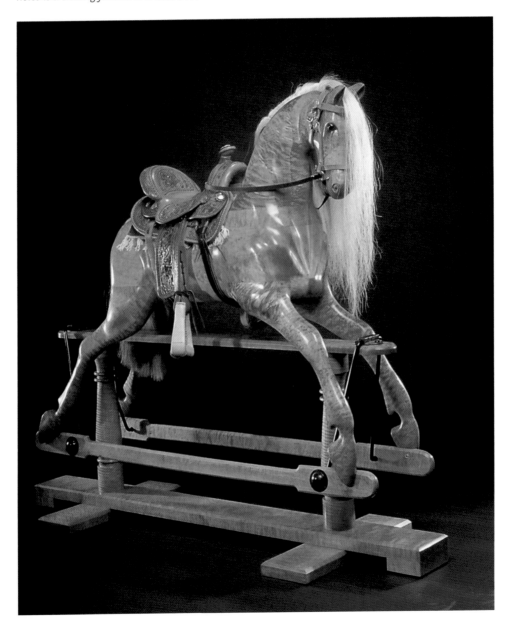

Bombay, Texas, *by Cream Pitcher Designs makes a strong statement to all guests with all of its curves and brands.*

Screens are most often used to hide such necessary implements as fireplaces, corners, and unruly papers. They can be large or small, but they must be easy on the eyes, as of course they are there for a purpose. Carved, hammered, leaded, or draped screens are also an excuse to add a little mystery to a room or dimension to an open space.

Pawnee Screen by Justin Stuff.

Fireplace stand by Stephen Winer.

Yellowstone Table *by Grizzly Creek Log Builders.*

Small collectibles cabinet by Sampson Bog Studio.

Tiny details go a long way in this delicately balanced conversation piece that's perched on cascading burls.

Beaded Magazine Rack *by Marc Taggart & Company, with leatherwork by Bev and Phil Simpson.*

With a beautiful splash of color, nothing can compare to the impact that the Beaded Magazine Rack *has on the eye. It is made of inland Douglas fir and gold ox hide with beaded leggings from the Wasco Indians, circa 1940s or '50s.*

entries, doors, and patios

Conveying warmth, character, whimsy, and wit, entries create first impressions. Whether grand or discreet, simple or ornate, entries give clues to what may be found beyond the front door. They establish a mood from the first glimpse to the last good-bye. Western entries have always provided a little mystery and some good humor. Many used to hint at the occupation of the inhabitant. Furs, skins, and cowboy boots told the story of the wearer long before introductions were made. Today, entries sport wide porches, carved doors, elaborate stairs, short overhangs, and grand trusses. Some beg to be loitered on after you ring the doorbell; others encourage quick and decisive conversation before the raindrops dampen letters. The last impression always comes from the entry. Strange how that works.

Every door begs to be opened. How could it not? A door promises the potential of a welcoming smile, the sweet aroma of freshly baked cookies, or the friendly bark of a canine friend. Doors are fun. They can be heavy and intimidating or light and delicately carved. They can be studded with pieces of juniper, caught up in the movement of their twists, or paneled with tin and leather. A house may have a speakeasy door with a panel that can be opened so the caller may be seen and spoken to without opening the door. Glass adds translucency, a peek into what may be a grand adventure or perhaps just a teasing moment of light. Glass may be beveled, stained, etched, or nonexistent. Doors are the handshake of the home.

There is laughter tinkling in the night somewhere in the distance on the other side of the lake. It must be the house with the glorious patio complete with a fireplace of stone, soft chairs of bright leather, and laughter. Always laughter. Patios are essential in the West. Summer nights, snowball fights, and the northern lights are just a few of the things experienced on patios where a part of living is brought out-doors. Some patios neatly match their house; others depart into another land, giving their occupants a sense of adventure. Patios allow us to enjoy the sky, trees, and rumbling thunder of a spring shower. Patios give way to water, grass, and forest. They are the transition to the playground of nature—whether we'll be wishing upon shooting stars; watching winged friends lighting for tidbits after our noonday meal; or watching as marmots peer through the stone crevices of the patio, waiting for a clear path to the table.

Morpheus *by Bison Legacy.*

A brilliant hammock of soft bison leather strung between stanchions of brushed metal, streamlined yet comfortable, gentle but strong. Morpheus offers a perfect place for respite after a long hard play in the outdoors.

Montana patio by LaChance Builders.

This patio at dusk brings a sense of warmth and comfort to the descending darkness. It is a welcome addition to a western home that allows the owners to enjoy the outdoors with the protection from the sudden changes in weather that is so common in the Rockies.

Black-walnut doors by SAR Furniture.

Magnificent black-walnut doors, deeply carved with scenes inspired by the wilderness of Wyoming's Yellowstone National Park, make an eloquent entry piece for a home.

Home designed by Storey Architects and built by Alpine Log Homes.

A snow-covered Montana entry—perfect for leaving skis behind after a day exploring Alpine trails or contemplating the size of the snowflakes that drift on the breezes—promises sanctuary from the weather.

Welcome Home, Cowboys! Entry *on a LaChance Builders home in Montana. Glasswork by Myni Ferguson.*

A Montana home opens its arms to visitors but first asks them to wipe their feet before entering the abode beyond.

Foyer beyond Welcome Home, Cowboys! Entry.

The owners wanted the first glance inside their home to convey a fun, warm feeling. Westside Story is a life-size sculpture cast in resin and hand painted by artist Jack Dowd. The back end of the Chevy truck is complete with tailgate and bumper. The mural behind was painted on canvas then attached like wallpaper to complete the scene. The etched glass in the foyer was done by Myni Ferguson.

Home and patio by Ward Blake Architects.

A Wyoming home is bathed in the morning sun. Its spacious patio allows the occupants to celebrate the sun's rays and the water's tranquility. The patio follows the home from north to south so that the views of the mountain range beyond are visible and all of its elevations can be appreciated as the light changes with the day and season. The ever-rising plane of the home allows the occupants to fully embrace and appreciate the remarkable display of nature that the windows frame.

Home by architects Stephen Dynia and Lisa Carranza-Habib.

A home of concrete, steel, and wood is a resoundingly beautiful display of modern western architecture. The home offers 360-degree views of mountains and a beautiful transition back to nature. The Zen-like water feature leads you gently from the hard edge of modern architecture back to the wild grasses and flowers on the site. "The feature is like being on the ocean, listening to the water as it flows over the river rocks in the splash-down pool," says Lisa.

alternate spaces

The West, whether being celebrated geographically or in some far corner of the world, is a well of inspiration for many craftspeople. All western designers and artists periodically reach that point where they wipe their brow and say, "I've reached the zenith of my career creatively—for now," and then move on to another project that's just as taxing and creative as the last. Western craftspeople's fearless approach to designing is why the genre keeps evolving and growing, gathering speed, and blossoming again and again.

Gypsy Wagon by Lynn Sedar Arambel of Ranch Willow Furniture.

Spaces outside the home have not evaded the reach of western design. Campers, wagons, and commercial spaces have opened their doors (literally) and readily accepted this cutting-edge western genre. Now guests are treated to a western delicacy when they are led to their quarters outside of the main home near a gentle stream. Guests climb the stairs into a cozy and delicately outfitted Gypsy Wagon by Lynn Sedar Arambel.

OPPOSITE: *Detail of a simple eating area in the Gypsy Wagon.*

Illuminations of History *by Penrose Lighting as seen in Silver Star restaurant in Helena, Montana.*
Interior by Thompson Interior Associates.

Steve Blood designed a set of pendant lights and wall sconces for a Montana steak house that tells a tale
of a bygone era. Thirty-one in all, the shades are photos reproduced from late-1800s and early-1900s
photos. The fixtures are of varying sizes. This pendant light has a double-tier shade with leather lacing.

OPPOSITE: Driskell Dome *by Stanton Glass.*

As you step into the Driskill Hotel in Austin, Texas, you are not only met by the warm, lavish atmosphere but by a
magnificent dome of stained and leaded glass that holds court in the lobby in the center of a corridor of columns.
"The dome sets the tone for the entire Driskill experience," says the managing director, Jeffery Trigger.

Ward and Blake Architects
PO Box 10399
Jackson, WY 83002
307.733.6867
www.wardblakearchitects.com

BUILDERS

Alpine Log Homes, Inc.
266 Hwy. 93 N.
Victor, MT 59875
406.642.3451
www.alpineloghomes.com

Culhane Contracting
Joe Culhane
7300 N. Saddle Rd.
Prescott, AZ 86305
928.778.3496

Eisenhart Builders
4115 Whitefish Stage Rd.
Kalispell, MT 59901
406.257.9395

LaChance Builders, Inc.
204 Wisconsin Ave.
Whitefish, MT 59937
406.862.5597
info@lachancebuilders.com
www.lachancebuilders.com

Preschutti Construction
Alan Preschutti
PO Box 7896
Mammoth Lakes, CA 93546
760.934.8466

RAM Construction
PO Box 4339
Jackson, WY 83001
307.733.4482
www.ram-construction.com

Schlauch Bottcher Construction, Inc.
Mike Schlauch
2010 Gilkerson
Bozeman, MT 59715
406.585.0735
mike@sbconstruction.com
www.sbconstruction.com

CABINETRY

Grand Woodworks
Jack and Karin Conrad
PO Box 748
Tabernash, CO 80478
970.726.5320
www.grandwoodworks.com

North Country Woodworks
Chris Neill
2555 Graves Creek Rd.
Eureka, MT 59917
406.889.3950
www.northcountryworks.com

Woodworks
455 Rhodes Draw
Kalispell, MT 59901
406.752.2399

CERAMIC WORK

Benedikt Strebel Ceramics
Benedikt Strebel
978 Guerrero St.
San Francisco, CA 94110
415.824.7949
bstrebel@sbcglobal.net
www.strebelceramics.com

Thirsty Lake Tileworks
Sarah Anderson
PO Box 538
Eureka, MT 59917
406.889.5324

FURNITURE

ANTLER FURNITURE
MacPhail's Studio
Danial S. MacPhail
5544 Hwy. W.
Poplar Bluff, MO 63901
573.686.1406
info@macphailstudio.com
www.macphailstudio.com

Nordberg Furniture
Doug Nordberg
PO Box 1763
Cody, WY 82414
307.587.3717

CONTEMPORARY WESTERN FURNITURE
Amber Jean, LLC
Amber Jean
1106 West Park #268
Livingston, MT 59047
406.222.9251
amber@amberjean.com
www.amberjean.com

Jeff Benedetto
65 St. Charles Ave.
San Francisco, CA 94132
415.334.9190
jeffben@sbcglobal.net

Blockhorse Designs, Inc.
Troy Evans
4302 Hwy. 87 S.
Roundup, MT 59072
406.323.2027
blockhorse@hotmail.com

Carl Dern Studio
Carl Dern
58 Park Rd.
Fairfax, CA 94930
415.457.1883
carl@dernstudio.com
www.carldernstudio.com

Chajo
Chanin Cook and Jonathan Edie
451 Montecito Blvd.
Napa, CA 94559
707.257.3676
info@chajo.com
www.chajo.com

COCOPA, Inc.
PO Box 2138
Evergreen, CO 80437
303.670.0684
www.cocopa.com

Mike Hemry
930 Canyon Ave.
Cody, WY 82414
307.587.8135
mhemry@wtp.net
www.michaelhemry.com

J. K. Brand Custom Designs
Jennifer King
4031 Green Busch Rd.
Katy, TX 77494
281.392.9261
jk@jkbrand.com
www.jkbrand.com

Kristian Brundsale Studio
Ed and Diane Grunseth
24 Horse Creek Rd. North Fork
Wilsall, MT 59086
406.578.9663
grunsethx2@imt.net
www.kristianbrunsdale.com

Mark Koons, Woodworker
Mark Koons
1356 Maple St.
Wheatland, WY 82201
307.322.2127
mkoons@wyoming.com

**Pat Olson Sculpture
and Furniture Art**
Pat Olson
812 Kimball Ave., Unit C
Grand Junction, CO 81501
970.245.3055
patolsonart@bresnan.net

Quandary Design, Inc.
Greg Race
408 W. 3rd St.
Leadville, CO 80461
719.486.3498
mail@quandarydesign.com
www.quandarydesign.com

R. Dana Merrill Designs
R. Dana Merrill
PO Box 824
Salmon, ID 83467
208.756.6660
merrills@salmoninternet.com
www.danamerrill.com

SAR Furniture, LLC
Scott A. Reitman
1420 E. 36th St., 6th Fl.
Cleveland, OH 44114
216.426.9990
scott@sarfurniture.com
www.sarfurniture.com

Spear S. Woodworks
Eric Shell
PO Box 438
Upton, WY 82730
307.272.7892

Stephen Winer Design
Stephen Winer
PO Box 113
Timnath, CO 80547
970.221.2470
winer@frii.com
www.stephenwiner.net

**Struempler Furniture
and Marquetry Art**
David Struempler
2251 Delores Way #5
Carbondale, CO 81623
970.379.2999
struempler@sopris.net

Unique Mesquite Furniture
Will Bogert
PO Box 387
Hondo, TX 78861
210.364.4498
www.uniquemesquite.com

Walker Woodworks
Earl M. Walker Jr.
206 E. 6th St.
Leadville, CO 80461
719.486.8284
walkerwoodworks@mindspring.com
www.walkerwoodworks.com

GAME TABLES
Grizzly Creek Billiards
Jeff Murphy
22071 Opal Rd.
Eckert, CO 81418
970.835.4682
jeff@grizzlycreek.com
www.grizzlycreek.com

LEATHER FURNITURE
Bison Legacy Gallery
Yazmhil and Brice Corman
10 Sage Dr.
Cody, WY 82414
307.587.4199
bisonlegacy@vcn.com
www.bisonlegacy.com

Chapman Design, Inc.
Christina Chapman
0075 Deer Trail Ave.
Carbondale, CO 81623
970.963.9580

Custom Leather Saddlery
Rick and Rhonda Yocham
Rt. 1 Box 536 A
Bartlesville, OK 74003
918.335.2277

Northwest Native Designs
Ernie Apondaca
182101-59th Ave. SE
Snohomish, WA 98296
800.322.3599
www.northwestnative.com

NATIONAL FURNITURE MANUFACTURERS
Century Furniture Industries
401-11th St. NW
Hickory, NC 28601
828.328.1851
www.centuryfurniture.com

Drexel Heritage Furniture Ind., Inc.
1925 Eastchester Dr.
High Point, NC 27265
336.888.4800
customerservice@drexelheritage.com
www.drexelheritage.com

Old Hickory Furniture
403 S. Noble St.
Shelbyville, IN 46176
800.232.2275
www.oldhickory.com

RETAIL FURNITURE
Brumbaugh's Leather Gallery
11651 Camp Bowie West
Fort Worth, TX 76008
817.244.9377
info@brumbaughs.com
www.brumbaughs.comCopper

Copper Creek Canyon
Lana Williams
3953 E. 82nd St.
Indianapolis, IN 46240
317.577.2990
customerservice@coppercreek
    canyon.com
www.coppercreekcanyon.com

Montana Homefitters
Sandee Fred
4949 Buckhouse Ln.
Missoula, MT 59804
406.541.8200
sales@homefitters.net
www.homefitters.net

Watauga Creek
25 Setser Branch Rd.
Franklin, NC 28734
800.443.1131
sales@wataugacreek.com
www.wataugacreek.com

RUSTIC FURNITURE
Adirondack Rustics Gallery
Darlene and Barry Gregson
739 Rt. 9
Schroon Lake, NY 12870
518.532.0020
info@adirondackrusticsgallery.com
www.adirondackrusticsgallery.com

Andy Sanchez Custom Furniture
Andy Sanchez
4 Archibeque Dr.
Algodones, NM 87001
505.385.1189
info@andysanchez.com
www.andysanchez.com

Big Creek Furniture
Dennis and M. J. Judd
South 15235 Canary Dr.
Strum, WI 54770
715.695.3318
big-creek@triwest.net

Covert Workshops
Jimmy Covert
2007 Public St.
Cody, WY 82414
307.527.5964

Escargot Fine Woodwork
Randy Edgar
88 Martin Ln.
Bellevue, ID 83313
208.578.0140

Fifield's, the Studio
Bill and Sandy Fifield
PO Box 366
Conifer, CO 80433
303.838.5072
macfifield@att.net

Russ Gleaves and Bill Coffey
PO Box 732
Northville, NY 12134
518.863.4602
wdc64@aol.com

Laramie River Designs
Gary Burditt
2721 Holly St.
Ft. Collins, CO 80526
970.472.9609
gary@laramieriverdesigns.com
www.laramieriverdesigns.com

Ryan Olson
230 Zemke Rd.
Talent, OR 97540
541.535.6859

Raven Haven
Michael, Colleen, and Joseph Brown
65495 Tweed Rd.
Bend, OR 97701
541.382.2576
mandcbrown@yahoo.com
www.ravenhavenfurniture.com

Rustic Furniture Limited Co.
Diane Ross
PO Box 253
Willow Creek, MT 59760
406.285.6882
diane@rusticfurniture.net

RusticStore.com
Jimmy Howard
10721-25th Ave. SW
Seattle, WA 98146
206.409.0229
jwrustic@earthlink.net
www.rusticstore.com

Sampson Bog Studio
Barney, Susan, and Erin Bellinger
Charley Brown
171 Paradise Pt.
Mayfield, NY 12117
518.661.6563

Santos Furniture
Lester Santos
PO Box 176
Cody, WY 82414
307.527.4407
www.santosfurniture.com

Wood River Rustics
Doug Tedrow
PO Box 3446
Ketchum, ID 83340
208.726.1442

WESTERN FURNITURE
Anne Beard
64209 Meadowbrook Rd.
Lexington, OR 97839
541.989.8144

Cream Pitcher Designs
Larry Cosens
418 Wapello St. N.
Mediapolis, IA 52637
319.394.3961

D. Rawlings and Sons, Inc.
Don Rawlings
PO Box 3100
Cody, WY 82414
307.527.6620
drawlings@wyoming.com

Fighting Bear Antiques
Terry Winchell
375 S. Cache
Jackson, WY 83001
307.733.2669
antiques@fightingbear.com
www.fightingbear.com

Greenwood Designs
Brad and Lorraine Greenwood
PO Box 164
Clio, CA 96106
530.836.0630
blgreenwood@neteze.com

R. C. Hink
PO Box 1142
Bellevue, ID 83313
208.788.6020
tonerihink@sunvalley.net
www.rchink.com

Hone's Design Studio
AL Hone
7254 S. 3200 W.
Benjamin, UT 84660
801.798.7555
honesdesign@msn.com
www.honesdesign.com

How Kola, LLC
Tim and Tiffany Lozier
507-16th St.
Cody, WY 82414
307.587.9814
howkola@wavecom.net
www.howkola.com

Into the West Gallery
PO Box 880767
Steamboat Springs, CO 80488
800.351.8377

L. D. Burke III Cowboy Furniture
L. D. Burke III
1105 Don Gaspar
Santa Fe, NM 87505
505.983.8001
ldburke@newmexico.com
www.ldburkeofsantafe.com

Legendary Heirloom
Jerry Van Vleet
3003 Keer Dam Rd.
Polson, MT 59860
406.883.3046
legheirloom@netscape.net

Marc Taggart and Co.
Marc Taggart
PO Box 1915
Cody, WY 82414
307.587.1800
marct@wtp.net
www.marctaggart.com

Mike Elliott Western Designs
Mike and Diane Elliott
PO Box 2465
Gardnerville, NV 89410
530.495.1069
info@westernfurniture.net
www.westernfurniture.net

Mortensen Studios
John Mortensen
PO Box 746
Wilson, WY 83014
307.733.1519
www.rainbowtrailcollection.com

New West
Matt and Venita Sheridan
2811 Big Horn Ave.
Cody, WY 82414
800.653.2391
msheridan@newwest.com
www.newwest.com

Norseman Designs West
John Gallis
38 Rd. 2AB
Cody, WY 82414
307.587.7777
jgallis@180com.net
www.norsemandesignswest.com

Ranch Willow Furniture Co.
Lynn Sedar Arambel
501 U.S. Highway 14 E.
Sheridan, WY 82801
307.674.1510

Renaissance West
Franco and Ann Guerri
PO Box 2037
Whitefish, MT 59937
406.892.8188
guerri@centurytel.net
www.rwmontana.com

Spotted Horse Studios
A. D. Sondra and Kate Tonnessen
202 Barsana Ave.
Austin, TX 78737
512.288.6266

Justin Stuff
Martha Cielesz
4721 Brookview Ave.
Rockford, IL 61107
815.397.4201
paddysquaw@insightbb.com

T. B. McCoy Western Designs
Tom McCoy
705 Rd. 1 AB
Clark, WY 82435
307.645.3331
mccoyfamily@nemontel.net

Texan Vintage Collection
Kathy Donegan
4898 CR 153
Bluff Dale, TX 76433
254.967.3190
info@texanvintagecollection.com
www.texanvintagecollection.com

Tim Groth Furniture
Tim Groth
PMB 158 111 Broadway, Ste. 133
Boise, ID 83702
208.338.0331
timgroth@timgrothfurniture.com
www.timgrothfurniture.com

Triangle Z Ranch Furniture
Ken Siggins
PO Box 995
Cody, WY 82414
307.587.3901

Western Heritage Furniture
Tim McClellan
PO Box 562
Jerome, AZ 86331
928.639.1424
mail@whf-inc.com
www.westernheritagefurniture.com

Wild West Designs, Inc.
Peter M. Fillerup
PO Box 286
Heber, UT 84032
435.654.4151
peter@wildwestdesigns.com
www.wildwestdesigns.com

Wildewood Furniture Co.
Ron and Jean Shanor
PO Box 1631
Cody, WY 82414
307.587.9558
www.wildewoodfurniture.com

GLASSWORK

Myni Ferguson
395 Blanchard Lake Dr.
Whitefish, MT 59937
406.862.5443
mferguson@cyberport.net

Stanton Glass Studio
Bryant Stanton
7781 Gholson Rd.
Waco, TX 76705
254.829.1151
info@stantonglass.com
www.stantonglass.com

Kate Tonnessen
624 Scott St.
Port Townsend, WA 98368
512.293.4424
shepardess_us@yahoo.com

INTERIOR DESIGNERS

G2
Gunnar Burkland
605 E. Dewey Pl.
San Antonio, TX 78212
210.737.2400

Harker Design
3465 N. Pines Way, Ste. 101
Wilson, WY 83014
307.733.5960
customerservice@harkerdesign.com
www.harkerdesign.com

Hilary Hemminway Interiors
Hilary Hemminway
140 Briar Patch Rd.
Stonington, CT 06378
860.535.4546

Marianne Bortz Interior Design, Inc.
PO Box 162
Fraser, CO 80442
970.726.9591
mbortz@direcway.com

Mary Margaret Interior Design
Mary Margaret
PO Box 1779
Big Fork, MT 59911

Sierra Design Studio
Robin Stater
PO Box 1280
Mammoth Lakes, CA 93546
760.934.4122
design@sierradesignstudio.com
www.sierradesignstudio.com

Snyder Design Group
Patti Snyder
1224 Ave. F
Billings, MT 59102
406.245.0785

Terry Hunziker, Inc.
Terry Hunziker
208-3rd Ave. S.
Seattle, WA 98104
206.467.1144

Thompson Interior Associates
Mitch Thompson, ASID
5432 Billy Casper Dr.
Billings, MT 59106
406.896.0688
mitchthompson@mitchthompson.com
www.mitchthompson.com

Velvet Leaf Studio
Barb Cooke
120 Park Ave.
Whitefish, MT 59937
406.862.4721
velvetleaf@centurytel.net

LIGHTING

Antler Art of the Plains
Larry Glaze
9313 County Dr. 175
Carthage, MO 64836
417.358.0753
www.antlerartoftheplains.com

Bill Feeley Art 'n' Iron
PO Box 2245
Cody, WY 82414
307.587.5194

Carl Dern Studio
Carl Dern
58 Park Rd.
Fairfax, CA 94930
415.457.1883
carl@dernstudio.com
www.carldernstudio.com

Dancing Light Lamps
Cloudbird
PO Box 1322
Twisp, WA 98856
509.997.2348
cloudbird@dancinglightlamps.com
www.dancinglightlamps.com

Dave LaMure Jr. Art Studio
Dave S. LaMure Jr.
3307 E. 3200 N.
Kimberly, ID 83441
208.736.0845
dave@davelamurejr.com
www.davelamurejr.com

DeCunzo Design Associates
Jason DeCunzo
508 Dixon Ave.
Missoula, MT 59801
406.542.1022
decunzo@montana.com
www.decunzodesign.com

Lean 2 Studio
John and Shirl Ireland-Stacy
PO Box 222
Adirondack, NY 12808
518.494.5185
mail@lean2.com
www.lean2.com

Penrose
Steve Blood
PO Box 295
Boston, NY 14025
716.941.0322
penrose@worldnet.att.net

Prairie Elk Forge
George F. Ainslie
PO Box 234
Lavina, MT 59046
406.636.2391

Roc Corbett Custom Lighting
Roc Corbett
PO Box 339
Big Fork, MT 59911
406.837.5823
rcorbett@centurytel.net
www.roccorbett.com

METALWORK

Archive Designs
Joseph Mross
3762 W. 11th Ave. #264
Eugene, OR 97402
541.607.6581
jmross@archivedesigns.com
www.archivedesigns.com

Art, Sand & Steel
Bert and Judy Hopple
2516 Mountain View Dr.
Cody, WY 82414
307.527.7861

Steve Fontanini
PO Box 1486
Jackson WY 83001
307.733.7668

Gilmore Metalsmithing Studio
Glenn F. Gilmore
PO Box 961
Hamilton, MT 59840
406.961.1861
glenn@gilmoremetal.com
www.gilmoremetal.com

Iron Mountain Forge
Marva Craft
680 Airfield Ln.
Sheridan, WY 82801
307.672.9220
marva@ironmountainforge.com
www.ironmountainforge.com

Joslyn Fine Metalwork
Steven J. Joslyn
1244 State Hwy. 80
Smyrna, NY 13464
800.985.9811
Steve@usblacksmith.com
www.usblacksmith.com

Knob Hill Forge
Gary Eagle
238 Hungry Hollow Rd.
Oroville, WA 98844
509.485.3853

Mike Dumas Copper Design
Mike Dumas
124 S. Otra Dr.
Ivins, UT 84738
435.673.5458
mike@mikedumascopper
  designs.com

John O'Hare
3690 Primrose Ave.
Santa Rosa, CA 95407
707.585.3589
johnlieo@earthlink.net
www.johnohare.com

John P. Simmons
Absarokee Blacksmith
PO Box 350
Absarokee, MT 59001
406.328.4311
absarokeeblacksmith@yahoo.com
www.absarokeeblacksmith.com

PORCELAIN

Reflections of Joi
Wantha Deaton
Rt. 4 Box 375
Broken Arrow, OK 74014
918.279.9049
www.reflectionsofjoi.com

SINKS

Crow's Feet, LLC
Julie Ann Patterson
PO Box 983
Gilbert, AZ 85299
480.329.7844
www.annorman.com

UPHOLSTERY

Robinson Upholstery
John Robinson
PO Box 743
Victor, ID 83455
208.787.2446

Thomas and Son Upholstery, Inc.
Cora and Michael Thomas
3645 Juniper Dr.
Helena, MT 59602
406.449.2314

photo credits

Ainslie, George, 103 (right)
Altman, Suzi, 116, 117

Bell, Phil, 58 (bottom), 152, 153
Bellinger, Barney, 79, 134
Benko Photography, 54
Bison Legacy Gallery, 136
Blood, Mary Lynn, 101 (bottom), 150
Boudreau, Josh, 76
Bryer, Stephen, 71 (top)
Buffalo Bill Historical Center, 24
   (image 1.69.6044.1,2)

Carr, Alan, 130
Century Furniture, 15, 17
Claussen, Chris, 8
Cobb, Elijah, 6 (both images), 7,
   10 (left), 14, 26 (bottom), 30, 39,
   42, 63, 67 (bottom left), 97, 101
   (top), 114, 115
Cold Snap Photography, 44
Cota, Deborah, 78

DeGabriele, 23, 35
Diggles, Warren, 108, 119, 132 (right)
Donaldson, Lynn, 60
Dowling, W. Garth, 127 (both)
Drexel Heritage Industries Ind., Inc., 16
Duckett, Gina, 106

Edgar, Randy, 89
Elliott, Mike, 55, 80
Emerald Bay Photography, 43, 52,
   59, 135

Greenwood, Brad, 121
Grizzly Creek Log Builders, 133
Grunseth, Diane, 118

Haddam, Jerry, 125
Hall, Audrey, 8, 12 (both), 13
Hecht, Pete, 62
Henrik, Kam, 58 (top)
Hone, Al, 5, 37, 120
Howard, Jimmy, 83

Jahiel, Adam, 20, 21, 38, 47 (both),
   74, 126, 148, 149
Jason Dewey Photography, 113
Josyln, Steve, 102

Kennard, Charles, 7 (bottom), 26
   (top), 61, 98

Lawrence, J. K., 94, 110, 141, 143
Line of the Spirit, 122
Living Images, back cover, 11, 40,
   99, 128, 138, 142
Livingstone, David, 92, 93
Long, Heidi, 82
Love, Richard, 106 (bottom)

MacPhail Studios, 56, 106 (top)
Maier, Ron, 51, 53, 57, 66
Marlow, David O., 32, 33, 81
McNabb Studio, 48 (bottom), 50
Merrill, R. Dana, 88
Michael Cooke Photography, 70
mike.com, 13
Morning Light Photography, 18, 19,
   25, 71 (bottom), 104

Nelson, Angie, 124 (bottom)

Orr's Photography, 131

Pearl, Robert, 2, 22
Pitken, Steve, 132 (left)
Pizzi+Thompson, 10 (right), 27, 100
PVC, 36 (top)

Sakwa, Hap, 67 (bottom right)
Salvat, Marjatta, 124 (top)
Sanchez, Andy, 90
SAR Furniture, 65, 140
Stanton Glass, 107, 151
Swift, David J., 72
Syms, Kevin, 36 (bottom), 48 (top),
   103 (left)

Tanner, Craig, 9
Tedrow, Doug, 67 (top)
Turley, Matthew, 77, 91, 96

Valainis, E. Anthony, 49
Van Inwegen, Bruce, back cover flap,
   105
Van Vleet, Jerry, 34

Wade, Roger, 46, 64, 69, 84, 85, 86,
   87, 112, 144, 147
Warchol, Paul, front cover, 28, 29
Wolfe, Supaya Gray, 123